Essential Guide to Writing

Writing Avenue

Rachel Somer

Paragraph Writing

3

DARAKWON

About the Author

Rachel Somer

BA in English Literature, York University, Toronto, Canada

Award-winning essayist, TOEIC developer, and author of educational books

Over ten years of experience as an English as a Second Language instructor

The author of *Fundamental Reading* Basic 1 and 2

—— **Essential Guide to Writing** ——

Writing Avenue 3
Paragraph Writing

Publisher Chung Kyudo
Author Rachel Somer
Editors Jeong Yeonsoon, Kim Mina, Seo Jeong-ah, Kim Mikyeong
Designers Park Narae, Forest

First published in February 2021
By Darakwon, Inc.
Darakwon Bldg., 211, Munbal-ro, Paju-si, Gyeonggi-do 10881
Republic of Korea
Tel: 82-2-736-2031 (Ext. 250)
Fax: 82-2-732-2037

ISBN 978-89-277-0449-2 54740
　　　 978-89-277-0446-1 54740 (set)

www.darakwon.co.kr

Photo Credits
Michkasova Elena (p. 11), Frederic Legrand - COMEO (p. 12), Paolo Bona (p. 14), Iurii Osadchi (p. 14), Vivida Photo PC (p. 14), mark reinstein (p. 14), Natursports (p.14), Tinseltown (p. 14), Alessia Pierdomenico (p. 14), Travers Lewis (p. 84) / www.shutterstock.com
File: Anne of Green Gables.jpg (p. 84) / https://commons.wikimedia.org

Components Main Book / Workbook
11 10 9 8 7 6 5　　24 25 26 27 28

Essential Guide to Writing

Writing Avenue

Paragraph Writing

3

Table of Contents

Unit	Topic	Writing Goal	Type of Writing
Unit 1	My Role Model	Write about your role model.	Descriptive Writing » Presentation
Unit 2	I Have a Bad Habit	Write about your bad habit.	Narrative Writing » Diary
Unit 3	A Restaurant Review	Write a review of a restaurant you went to.	Descriptive Writing » Review
Unit 4	I Have a Problem	Write about how to solve a problem.	Expository Writing » Letter
Unit 5	My Favorite Musical Genre	Write about your favorite musical genre.	Descriptive Writing » Blog
Unit 6	My Favorite Holiday	Write about your favorite holiday.	Expository Writing » Email
Unit 7	Volunteering	Write about volunteering.	Narrative Writing » Report
Unit 8	My Book Report	Write about a book you read.	Expository Writing » Book Report

Vocabulary	Grammar	Page
jobs and achievements	• relative pronoun *who* • as a result	10
bad habits and solutions	• will • instead of	20
types of restaurants, foods, and tastes	• both *A* and *B* • make + object + verb	30
common teen problems and advice	• how to + verb • had better + verb	40
musical genres and the moods they create	• passive: be + p.p. + by • If you ~, why don't you ~?	50
holidays and holiday traditions around the world	• gerund (verb-ing) as a subject • relative pronoun *that*	60
places to volunteer and volunteer activities	• much + comparative adjective • although + subject + verb	70
character and book descriptions	• past participle • adjective + to-infinitive	80
Vocabulary & Structure Review		91

How to Use This Book

• Student Book

1. Before You Write

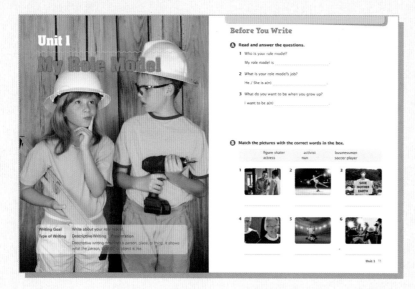

Thinking about the Topic

Three warm-up questions help students think about the writing topic.

Previewing the Key Vocabulary

Students can learn the key vocabulary by matching the words with the pictures or filling in the table.

2. Understanding the Model Text

Reading the Model Text

Students can read an example of the writing topic and use it as a template when they write their passage.

Completing the Graphic Organizer

By completing the graphic organizer, students can learn the structure of the model text. This also helps them organize their writing.

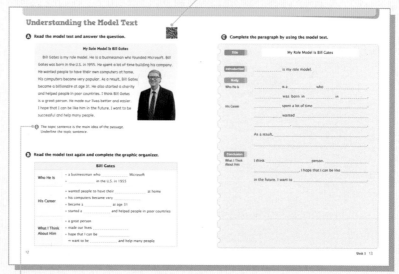

QR code for listening to the model text

A question about the model text is provided.

Completing the Paragraph

By completing the paragraph, students can review the model text and learn what the passage consists of.

3. Collecting Ideas

Getting Ideas from Collecting Ideas

Ideas related to the writing topic are provided. Students can brainstorm and learn new ideas before writing their draft.

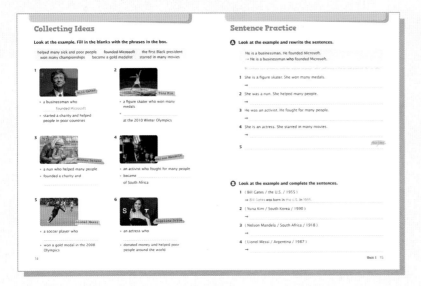

4. Sentence Practice

Practicing Sentences with Key Structures

Various types of questions allow students to practice the key structures of the model text. They also help students gather ideas before writing.

5. Sentence Practice Plus

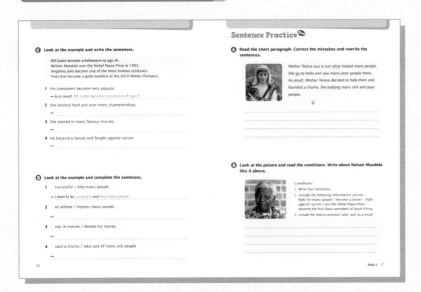

Correcting a Short Paragraph

Students can check if they understand the key structures they learned by correcting the mistakes in the short paragraph.

Writing a Short Paragraph

Students should write a short paragraph by using the given picture and the conditions. This helps students practice the key structures.

6. Brainstorming & First Draft

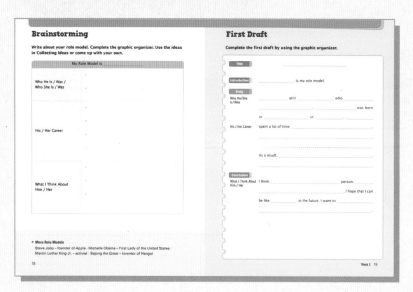

Brainstorming

By completing the graphic organizer, students can organize their ideas prior to writing the first draft.

First Draft

Students should complete the first draft by using the graphic organizer. They can revise, edit the first draft, and write the final draft in the workbook.

Vocabulary and Structure Review

Students can review the key vocabulary they learned in each unit by writing the meaning of each word and phrase. They can also review the key structures in the unit.

• Workbook

7. More Questions

Students can practice and review the key structures. They can also complete the model text by matching the phrases.

8. Revise & Edit → Final Draft

After writing the first draft, students can revise and edit the draft, and then write the final draft.

About Paragraph Writing

1. What Is a Paragraph?

A paragraph is a short piece of writing that handles a single idea or concept. All the sentences in a given paragraph should be related to a single topic. Paragraphs can stand alone, or they can be added to longer pieces of writing such as essays, stories, articles, and many more.

2. What Does a Paragraph Consist of?

A paragraph consists of a topic sentence, supporting details, and a concluding sentence.

– The topic sentence is the main idea of the passage.

– Supporting details are information and examples that explain the topic.

– The concluding sentence is the final thought of the passage.

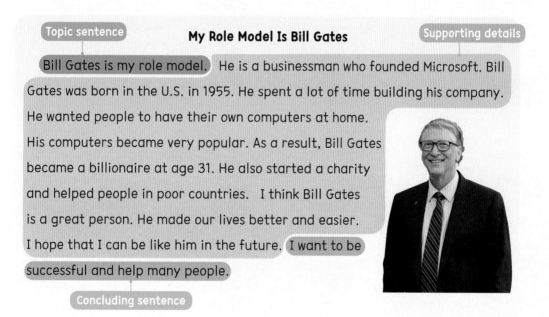

Topic sentence

My Role Model Is Bill Gates

Supporting details

Bill Gates is my role model. He is a businessman who founded Microsoft. Bill Gates was born in the U.S. in 1955. He spent a lot of time building his company. He wanted people to have their own computers at home. His computers became very popular. As a result, Bill Gates became a billionaire at age 31. He also started a charity and helped people in poor countries. I think Bill Gates is a great person. He made our lives better and easier. I hope that I can be like him in the future. I want to be successful and help many people.

Concluding sentence

3. What Are the Types of Paragraph Writing?

1) Expository Writing

It gives information about a topic or tells you how to do something.

2) Narrative Writing

It describes a story that happened to you. It can also describe imaginary events.

3) Persuasive Writing

It encourages a reader to make a choice by providing evidence and examples.

4) Descriptive Writing

It describes a person, place, or thing. It shows what the person, location, or object is like.

Unit 1
My Role Model

Writing Goal	Write about your role model.
Type of Writing	Descriptive Writing Presentation

Descriptive writing describes a person, place, or thing. It shows what the person, location, or object is like.

Before You Write

Ⓐ Read and answer the questions.

1 Who is your role model?

My role model is _____ .

2 What is your role model's job?

He / She is a(n) _____ .

3 What do you want to be when you grow up?

I want to be a(n) _____ .

Ⓑ Match the pictures with the correct words in the box.

figure skater	activist	businessman
actress	nun	soccer player

1

_____

2

_____

3

SAVE MOTHER EARTH

_____

4

_____

5

_____

6

_____

Understanding the Model Text

A Read the model text and answer the question.

My Role Model Is Bill Gates

Bill Gates is my role model. He is a businessman who founded Microsoft. Bill Gates was born in the U.S. in 1955. He spent a lot of time building his company. He wanted people to have their own computers at home. His computers became very popular. As a result, Bill Gates became a billionaire at age 31. He also started a charity and helped people in poor countries. I think Bill Gates is a great person. He made our lives better and easier. I hope that I can be like him in the future. I want to be successful and help many people.

Q The topic sentence is the main idea of the passage. Underline the topic sentence.

B Read the model text again and complete the graphic organizer.

Bill Gates	
Who He Is	• a businessman who _____ Microsoft • _____ in the U.S. in 1955
His Career	• wanted people to have their _____ at home • his computers became very _____ • became a _____ at age 31 • started a _____ and helped people in poor countries
What I Think About Him	• a great person • made our lives _____ • hope that I can be _____ → want to be _____ and help many people

G **Complete the paragraph by using the model text.**

| Title | My Role Model Is Bill Gates |

Introduction

_____ is my role model.

Body

Who He Is

_____ is a _____ who _____.

_____ was born in _____ in _____.

His Career

_____ spent a lot of time _____.

_____ wanted _____.

_____. _____.

As a result, _____.

_____.

Conclusion

What I Think
About Him

I think _____ person. _____

_____. I hope that I can be like _____

in the future. I want to _____.

Collecting Ideas

Look at the example. Fill in the blanks with the phrases in the box.

helped many sick and poor people   ~~founded Microsoft~~   the first Black president
won many championships   became a gold medalist   starred in many movies

1

Bill Gates

- a businessman who

  founded Microsoft

- started a charity and helped people in poor countries

2

Yuna Kim

- a figure skater who won many medals

- _____

  at the 2010 Winter Olympics

3

Mother Teresa

- a nun who helped many people

- founded a charity and

  _____

4

Nelson Mandela

- an activist who fought for many people

- became _____

  of South Africa

5

Lionel Messi

- a soccer player who

  _____

- won a gold medal in the 2008 Olympics

6

Angelina Jolie

- an actress who

  _____

- donated money and helped poor people around the world

Sentence Practice

A **Look at the example and rewrite the sentences.**

He is a businessman. He founded Microsoft.
→ He is a businessman **who** founded Microsoft.

🖋 Combine two sentences with the relative pronoun "who" and remove the second pronoun "he" or "she."

1 She is a figure skater. She won many medals.

➡ _____

2 She was a nun. She helped many people.

➡ _____

3 He was an activist. He fought for many people.

➡ _____

4 She is an actress. She starred in many movies.

➡ _____

Your Idea

5 _____

B **Look at the example and complete the sentences.**

1 (Bill Gates / the U.S. / 1955)

➡ Bill Gates **was born in** the U.S. **in** 1955. _____

2 (Yuna Kim / South Korea / 1990)

➡ _____

3 (Nelson Mandela / South Africa / 1918)

➡ _____

4 (Lionel Messi / Argentina / 1987)

➡ _____

C **Look at the example and write the sentences.**

> ~~Bill Gates became a billionaire at age 31.~~
> Nelson Mandela won the Nobel Peace Prize in 1993.
> Angelina Jolie became one of the most famous actresses.
> Yuna Kim became a gold medalist at the 2010 Winter Olympics.

1 His computers became very popular.

→ **As a result,** Bill Gates became a billionaire at age 31.

2 She worked hard and won many championships.

→ _____

3 She starred in many famous movies.

→ _____

4 He became a lawyer and fought against racism.

→ _____

D **Look at the example and complete the sentences.**

1 | successful / help many people |

→ **I want to be** successful **and** help many people.

2 | an athlete / impress many people |

→ _____

3 | star in movies / donate my money |

→ _____

4 | start a charity / take care of many sick people |

→ _____

Sentence Practice Plus

A Read the short paragraph. Correct the mistakes and rewrite the sentences.

Mother Teresa was a nun <u>what</u> helped many people. She <u>go</u> to India and saw many poor people there. As <u>result</u>, Mother Teresa decided to help them and founded a charity. She <u>helping</u> many sick and poor people.

_____

_____

_____

_____

B Look at the picture and read the conditions. Write about Nelson Mandela like A above.

Conditions

① Write four sentences.

② Include the following information: activist – fight for many people / become a lawyer – fight against racism / win the Nobel Peace Prize / become the first Black president of South Africa.

③ Include the relative pronoun "who" and "as a result."

_____

_____

_____

_____

Brainstorming

Write about your role model. Complete the graphic organizer. Use the ideas in Collecting Ideas or come up with your own.

My Role Model Is _____	
Who He Is / Was / Who She Is / Was	• •
His / Her Career	• • • •
What I Think About Him / Her	• • •

♦ **More Role Models**

Steve Jobs – founder of Apple / Michelle Obama – First Lady of the United States / Martin Luther King Jr. – activist / Sejong the Great – inventor of Hangul

First Draft

Complete the first draft by using the graphic organizer.

Title _____

Introduction _____ is my role model.

Body

Who He/She Is/Was

_____ a(n) _____ who _____

_____. _____ was born

in _____ in _____. _____

His / Her Career spent a lot of time _____.

_____.

_____.

As a result, _____.

_____.

Conclusion

What I Think About Him / Her I think _____ person. _____

_____. I hope that I can

be like _____ in the future. I want to _____

_____.

Unit 2

I Have a Bad Habit

Writing Goal	Write about your bad habit.
Type of Writing	Narrative Writing Diary
	Narrative writing describes a story that happened to you. Narrative writing can also describe imaginary events.

Before You Write

A **Read and answer the questions.**

1 Do you have any bad habits?

☐ Yes, I do. ☐ No, I don't.

2 What is your bad habit?

My bad habit is _____.

3 How do you feel about your bad habit?

I _____.

B **Match the pictures with the correct phrases in the box.**

tap my feet   bite my nails   play with my phone
eat fast food   stay up too late   play with my hair

1

_____

2

_____

3

_____

4

_____

5

_____

6

_____

Understanding the Model Text

A Read the model text and answer the question.

My Bad Habit: Biting My Nails

Dear Diary,

I have a terrible habit. These days, I always bite my nails. I started doing this because I was stressed out. My teacher said I should stop doing it, so I made a plan. First, I will put tape around my fingers. When I feel stressed, I will bite the tape instead. This will remind me to stop biting my nails. Second, I will practice some healthy habits. Instead of biting my nails, I will take deep breaths. Then I will feel calm and relaxed. I will also start exercising regularly. It won't be easy, but I am sure I can break my bad habit!

Q The concluding sentence is the final thought of the passage.
Underline the concluding sentence.

B Read the model text again and complete the graphic organizer.

My Bad Habit		
What My Habit Is		• always _____ • because I _____
My Plan to Stop It	First	• _____ around my fingers • _____ the tape instead → remind me to _____ my nails
	Second	• practice some _____ • take _____ → feel calm and relaxed • also start _____

22

C **Complete the paragraph by using the model text.**

| Title | My Bad Habit: Biting My Nails |

Introduction

Dear Diary,

I have a terrible habit.

Body

What My Habit Is

These days, I _____. I started doing this

because _____. My _____ said

First Plan

I should stop _____, so I made a plan. First, I will

_____. When I feel _____,

I will _____. This will _____

Second Plan

_____. Second, I _____

_____. Instead of _____,

I will _____. Then I _____

_____. I will also _____.

Conclusion

It won't be easy, but I am sure I can _____ my bad habit!

Collecting Ideas

Look at the example. Fill in the blanks with the phrases in the box.

~~put tape around my fingers~~	tie my hair back	stop eating late at night
stop eating snacks	stretch when I feel restless	stop using my phone

1

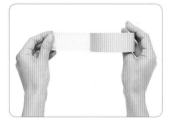

- Bite my nails
- _put tape around my fingers_
- practice some healthy habits

2

- Play with my hair
- _____
- learn how to calm myself

3

- Play with my phone
- _____

  during meals
- set a timer when I use my phone

4

- Eat fast food
- eat more healthy foods
- _____

  when I'm bored

5

- Stay up too late
- _____
- listen to relaxing music

6

- Tap my feet
- exercise every morning
- _____

Sentence Practice

A **Look at the example and rewrite the sentences.**

> I am stressed out.
> → I **started doing this because** I **was** stressed out.

1 I am worried.

→ _____

2 I am nervous.

→ _____

3 I am bored.

→ _____

Your Idea

4 _____

B **Look at the pictures. Complete the sentences with the phrases in the box.**

stop eating snacks when I'm bored   ~~put tape around my fingers~~
listen to relaxing music   exercise every morning

1
First, I will put tape around my fingers.

Second, I will practice some healthy habits.

2
First, I will eat more healthy foods.

_____

3
_____

Second, I will stretch when I feel restless.

4
First, I will stop eating late at night.

_____

C Look at the example and complete the sentences.

1 (feel stressed / bite the tape instead)

→ **When I** feel stressed, **I will** bite the tape instead.

2 (feel hungry / eat fruits, vegetables, and healthy meats)

→ _____

3 (have dinner / leave my phone in my room)

→ _____

D Look at the pictures. Complete the sentences with the phrases in the box.

take deep breaths	stand up and stretch
play with my dog	put on some slow songs

💡 Remember to add a gerund (verb-ing) after "instead of."

1 (bite my nails)

→ **Instead of biting** my nails, **I will** take deep breaths.

2 (eat)

→ _____

3 (play with my hair)

→ _____

4 (watch TV)

→ _____

E Look at the example and complete the sentences.

1 calm and relaxed → **Then I will feel** calm and relaxed.

2 not / bored anymore → _____

3 not / nervous or stressed → _____

Sentence Practice ^{Plus}

A **Read the short paragraph. Correct the mistakes and rewrite the sentences.**

These days, I always play with my phone. First, I <u>stop</u> using a phone during meals. Second, I will <u>setting</u> a timer when I use my phone. Instead <u>at</u> playing for hours, I will use my phone for thirty minutes.

_____

_____

_____

_____

B **Look at the picture and read the conditions. Write about a bad habit like A above.**

Conditions

① Write four sentences.

② Include the following information: tap my feet / exercise every morning / stretch – feel restless / stand up and stretch.

③ Include "will" and "instead of."

_____

_____

_____

_____

Brainstorming

Write about your bad habit. Complete the graphic organizer. Use the ideas in Collecting Ideas or come up with your own.

My Bad Habit: _____	
What My Habit Is	• •
My Plan to Stop It	First: • • → Second: • • → •

✦ **More Bad Habits**

losing my things / forgetting my homework / picking my nose / interrupting my friends / breaking my promises

First Draft

Complete the first draft by using the graphic organizer.

Title _____

Introduction

Dear Diary,

I have a terrible habit.

Body

What My Habit Is

These days, I _____. I started doing

this because I _____. My _____ said

First Plan

I should stop _____, so I made a plan. First,

I _____. When I _____,

I _____.

This will _____.

Second Plan

Second, I _____. Instead of

_____, I will _____.

Then I _____. I will also

_____.

Conclusion

It won't be easy, but I am sure I can _____ my bad habit!

Unit 3

A Restaurant Review

Writing Goal	Write a review of a restaurant you went to.
Type of Writing	Descriptive Writing » Review
	Descriptive writing describes a person, place, or thing. It shows what the person, location, or object is like.

Before You Write

A **Read and answer the questions.**

1 Do you like to eat at restaurants?

☐ Yes, I do. ☐ No, I don't.

2 What is your favorite restaurant?

My favorite restaurant is _____.

3 What do you usually order?

I usually order _____.

B **Fill in the chart with the words in the box.**

pasta	creamy	spicy	steak
sushi rolls	fresh	noodles	crunchy

Foods	Descriptions
• _____	• _____
• _____	• _____
• _____	• _____
• _____	• _____

Understanding the Model Text

A Read the model text and answer the question.

Review: Teddy's Grill House ★ ★ ★ ★   January 17

I ate at Teddy's Grill House last week with my mom. We ordered steak, cream pasta, and a salad. Both the steak and the cream pasta tasted amazing. The steak was fresh, and the pasta was hot and creamy. However, the salad was very small and expensive. For dessert, we had chocolate cake. It was sweet and fluffy. The service was very good. I thought the waiter was funny, and he made us laugh. Unfortunately, the restaurant was very noisy. The music was just too loud. All in all, Teddy's Grill House is a great place to eat. I recommend the steak!

Q The concluding sentence is the final thought of the passage. Underline the concluding sentence.

B Read the model text again and complete the graphic organizer.

Teddy's Grill House	
The Food	• steak – fresh • cream pasta – hot and _____ • salad – very small and _____ • chocolate cake – _____
The Service	• very good • waiter was funny – he _____
The Restaurant	• very noisy • music was just _____
My Opinion	recommend the _____

C **Complete the paragraph by using the model text.**

Title

Review: Teddy's Grill House

Introduction

When I Went There

I ate at _____ with my _____.

Body

The Food

We ordered _____. Both _____

_____ and _____ tasted _____.

The _____, and _____.

However, _____.

For dessert, we had _____. _____

The Service

_____. The service was _____.

I thought _____, and _____

The Restaurant

made us _____. _____, the restaurant was

_____. _____.

Conclusion

My Opinion

All in all, _____ is _____

place to eat. I recommend _____!

Collecting Ideas

Look at the example. Fill in the blanks with the words and phrases in the box.

| spring rolls | apple pie | beef tacos | soft and sweet | ~~hot and creamy~~ |
| noodles | too oily | fresh and crunchy | crunchy and sweet |

1
Teddy's Grill House

- pasta: _hot and creamy_
- salad: small and expensive
- chocolate cake: sweet and fluffy

2
Jin's Sushi House

- sushi rolls: fresh
- _____: hot and spicy
- fried rice: _____

3
Country Burger Hut

- hamburgers: juicy
- pasta salad: bland and oily
- _____: warm and soft

4
May's Barbecue

- pork: delicious
- tofu soup: bitter
- fruit salad: _____

5
Thai Extreme

- pad thai: amazing
- _____: hard and dry
- mango pudding: _____

6
Tastes of Mexico

- _____: wonderful
- nachos: too soft
- churros: _____

Sentence Practice

A **Look at the example and complete the sentences.**

1 Teddy's Grill House / last week / mom

→ **I ate at** Teddy's Grill House last week **with my** mom. _____

2 Jin's Sushi House / on Sunday / parents

→ _____

3 Country Burger Hut / last month / family

→ _____

4 Tastes of Mexico / three days ago / friend

→ _____

Your Idea

5 _____

B **Look at the example and rewrite the sentences.**

The steak tasted amazing. The cream pasta tasted amazing.

→ **Both** the steak **and** the cream pasta tasted amazing.

💡 Use "both A and B" to describe how two things are the same in quality, size, shape, etc.

1 The sushi rolls tasted great. The noodles tasted great.

→ _____

2 The hamburgers tasted delicious. The French fries tasted delicious.

→ _____

3 The pad thai tasted wonderful. The curry tasted wonderful.

→ _____

4 The beef tasted amazing. The pork tasted amazing.

→ _____

Your Idea

5 _____

C Look at the pictures. Complete the sentences with the phrases in the box.

~~salad / very small and expensive~~   nachos / too soft   fried rice / too oily

1 The pasta was hot and creamy.

However, the salad **was** very small and expensive.

2 The noodles were hot and spicy.

3 The chicken burritos were fresh.

D Look at the example and rewrite the sentences.

1 The waiter was funny. We laughed.

→ **I thought** the waiter was funny, **and he made us laugh**.

2 The waiter was rude. We waited for a long time.

→

3 The manager was kind. We smiled.

→

E Look at the example and complete the sentences.

💡 Use "unfortunately" for something negative. Use "fortunately" for something positive.

1 (very noisy) (music / just too loud)

→ **Unfortunately, the restaurant was** very noisy. **The** music **was** just too loud.

2 (very comfortable) (chairs / big and soft)

→

3 (uncomfortable) (tables / too small)

→

36

Sentence Practice Plus

A **Read the short paragraph. Correct the mistakes and rewrite the sentences.**

I eat at May's Barbecue on Saturday with my grandma. Both the pork but the beef tasted amazing. However, the tofu soup is bitter. I thought the manager was funny, and she made our laugh.

_____

_____

_____

B **Look at the picture and read the conditions. Write about Thai Extreme like A above.**

Conditions

① Write four sentences.

② Include the following information: yesterday – cousins / pad thai, curry – wonderful / spring rolls – hard and dry / waiter – rude, wait for a long time.

③ Include "both *A* and *B*" and "make + object + verb."

_____

_____

_____

_____

Brainstorming

Write a review of a restaurant you went to. Complete the graphic organizer. Use the ideas in Collecting Ideas or come up with your own.

Review: _____	
The Food	• • • •
The Service	• •
The Restaurant	• •
My Opinion	

• **More Foods**

  garlic bread / fried chicken / seaweed soup / dumplings / pork cutlet / pho

• **More Desserts**

  cheesecake / brownie / pudding / strawberry pie / cupcake / cookie / ice cream sandwich

First Draft

Complete the first draft by using the graphic organizer.

Title _____

Introduction

When I Went There

I ate at _____ with my _____

_____.

Body

The Food

We ordered _____. Both

_____ and _____ tasted _____.

The _____, and _____

_____. However, _____.

For dessert, we had _____. _____

The Service

_____. The service _____.

I thought _____, and _____ made

The Restaurant

us _____. _____, the restaurant was

_____. _____.

Conclusion

My Opinion

All in all, _____ is _____ place

to eat. I recommend _____!

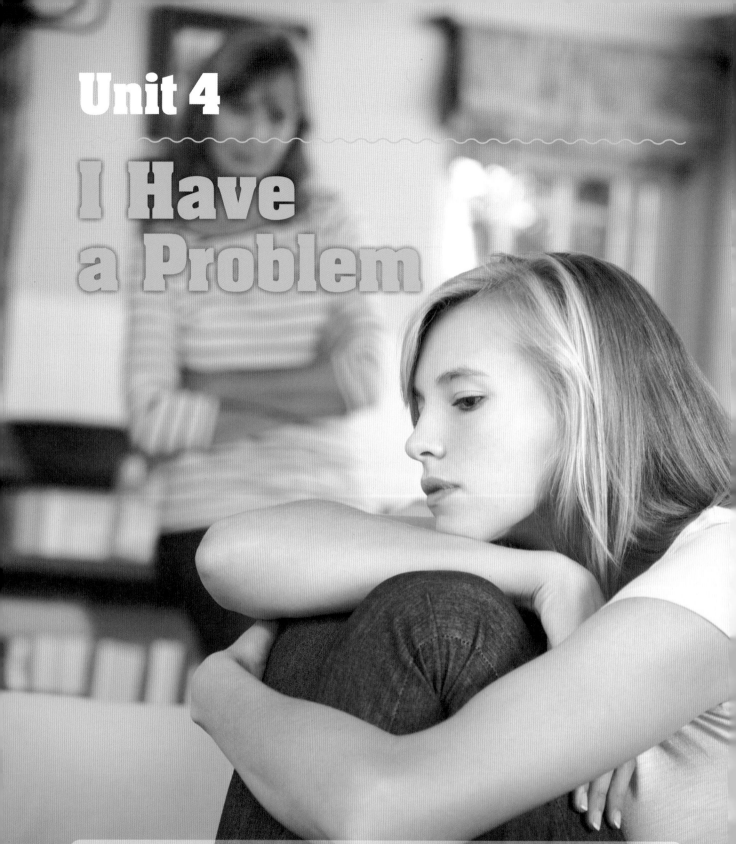

Unit 4

I Have a Problem

Writing Goal	Write about how to solve a problem.
Type of Writing	Expository Writing » Letter
	Expository writing gives information about a topic or tells you how to do something.

40

Before You Write

A **Read and answer the questions.**

1 Do you solve your problems easily?

☐ Yes, I do. ☐ No, I don't.

2 Do you give your friends advice?

☐ Yes, I do. ☐ No, I don't.

3 Who gives you advice?

_____ give(s) me advice.

B **Match the pictures with the correct phrases in the box.**

lose things	too shy	have acne
too clumsy	always late	don't have friends

1

2

3

_____

_____

_____

4

5

6

_____

_____

_____

Understanding the Model Text

A **Read the model text and answer the question.**

Dear Mr. Advice,

I have to do a presentation, but I'm too shy. Please tell me how to solve this!

Shy Susan

Dear Shy Susan,

You must feel bad about being shy. Most people are a little shy, so don't worry. Here are a few tips. First, practice your presentation often. Memorize the words and speak clearly. Second, many people feel nervous in front of a crowd. This can cause stress, so try to breathe deeply. If your shyness gets worse, you had better talk to someone. You can get advice from your teacher. Follow these tips, and you will be less shy!

Q What is the passage mainly about?
   a. why Susan feels shy
   b. how to be less shy

B **Read the model text again and complete the graphic organizer.**

I'm Too Shy		
Problem	• have to _____, but I'm too shy	
	• tell me _____	
Solution	First	• _____ your presentation _____
		• _____ and speak clearly
	Second	• many people _____ in front of a crowd
		→ can cause stress, so try to _____
If It Gets Worse	• _____	
	• _____ from your teacher	

C **Complete the paragraph by using the model text.**

Title	My Problem: I'm Too Shy

Introduction

Dear Mr. Advice,

Problem

I _____. Please tell me

_____!

_____

Body

Dear _____,

Solution

You must feel bad about _____. _____

_____, so don't worry. Here are

- First

_____. First, _____.

_____.

- Second

Second, many _____.

_____ can _____, so try to _____

If It Gets Worse

_____. If _____ gets worse, you had

better _____. You can _____

_____.

Conclusion

Follow these tips, and you will be _____!

Collecting Ideas

Look at the example. Fill in the blanks with the phrases in the box.

~~breathe deeply~~	write your schedule	write your name
wear comfortable shoes	join a sports team	wash your face

1

- I'm too shy to do a presentation:
- practice your presentation often
- try to ___breathe deeply___

2

- I have acne:
- _____ twice a day
- try to reduce your stress levels

3

- I'm too clumsy:
- _____
- pay attention outside

4

- I'm always late:
- wear a watch
- _____ on a calendar

5

- I always lose things at school:
- _____ on your things
- pack your bag slowly

6

- I don't have many friends:
- be friendly to your classmates
- _____

Sentence Practice

A **Look at the example and complete the sentences.**

> (tell me / solve / this)
> → **Please** tell me **how to** solve this!

💡 Use "how to" when writing about a method of doing something.

1 (tell me / cure / it)

→ _____

2 (tell me / fix / this)

→ _____

3 (tell me / make / friends)

→ _____

Your Idea

4 _____

B **Look at the example and write the sentences.**

> don't walk on slippery surfaces   ~~memorize the words and speak clearly~~
> don't wear too much makeup   remember to check the time regularly

1 First, practice your presentation often.

Memorize the words and speak clearly.

2 First, wash your face twice a day.

_____

3 First, wear comfortable shoes.

_____

4 First, wear a watch.

_____

C Look at the pictures. Complete the sentences with the phrases in the box.

~~try to breathe deeply~~	pack your bag slowly
try to reduce your stress levels	join a sports team

1 Second, many people feel nervous in front of a crowd.

This can cause stress, _____ **so** try to breathe deeply _____.

2 Second, many teens get stressed out easily.

Stress can cause acne, _____.

3 Second, many students enjoy sports.

Sports can help you meet people, _____.

4 Second, many students are in a hurry.

This can make you forget things, _____.

D Look at the example and complete the sentences.

💡 Use "had better" to recommend someone do something.

1 shyness gets worse → talk to someone

→ **If your** shyness gets worse, **you had better** talk to someone.

2 acne gets worse → see a doctor

→ _____

3 problem gets worse → talk to your parents

→ _____

4 clumsiness gets worse → try yoga

→ _____

Sentence Practice Plus

A **Read the short paragraph. Correct the mistakes and rewrite the sentences.**

A: I am always late. Please tell me <u>how</u> fix this!

B: First, <u>wearing</u> a watch.

Second, <u>to write</u> your schedule on a calendar.

If your problem gets worse, you <u>have better</u> talk to your teacher.

_____

_____

_____

_____

B **Look at the picture and read the conditions. Write about how to solve a problem like A above.**

Conditions

① Write five sentences.

② Include the following information: always lose my things at school / write your name on your things / pack your bag slowly / talk to your parents.

③ Include "how to + verb" and "had better."

_____

_____

_____

_____

Brainstorming

Write about how to solve a problem. Complete the graphic organizer. Use the ideas in Collecting Ideas or come up with your own.

My Problem: _____		
Problem	• •	
Solution	**First**	• •
	Second	• →
If It Gets Worse	• •	

More Problems

I often fight with my friend. / I'm bad at sports. / I always forget my homework. / My test scores are bad.

First Draft

Complete the first draft by using the graphic organizer.

Title

_____

Introduction

Dear Mr. Advice,

Problem

I _____. Please tell me

_____!

_____

Body

Dear _____,

Solution

You must feel bad about _____. _____

_____, so don't worry. Here are

- First

_____. First, _____.

_____.

- Second

Second, _____.

_____ can _____, so _____

If It Gets Worse

_____. If _____ gets worse,

you had better _____. You can

_____.

Conclusion

Follow these tips, and _____ will be _____!

Unit 5
My Favorite Musical Genre

Writing Goal   Write about your favorite musical genre.

Type of Writing   Descriptive Writing 》 Blog

Descriptive writing describes a person, place, or thing. It shows what the person, location, or object is like.

Before You Write

A **Read and answer the questions.**

1 Do you like to listen to music?

☐ Yes, I do.   ☐ No, I don't.

2 What is your favorite musical genre?

I like _____ best.

3 Who is your favorite singer or group?

I like _____ best.

B **Fill in the chart with the words in the box.**

smooth	jazz	upbeat	classical
rock	pop	relaxing	loud

Musical Genres	Descriptions
• _____	• _____
• _____	• _____
• _____	• _____
• _____	• _____

Understanding the Model Text

A Read the model text and answer the question.

I Like Pop Music Best

I like many types of music, but my favorite genre is pop. I learned about pop music from my sister. Pop music is performed by a singer or a group. There are singers and dancers in the group. The songs are usually fast and upbeat. I always listen to pop music on the bus in the morning. The music makes me feel happy. I listen to it until I get to school. When I exercise after school, I dance to my favorite songs. They help me relieve stress after a long day. If you like cheerful music, why don't you listen to pop?

Q What is the passage mainly about?
a. why the author likes pop music
b. what pop music sounds like

B Read the model text again and complete the graphic organizer.

Pop Music	
How I Learned About It	from _____
About the Genre	• _____ by a singer or a group • singers and dancers in the group • songs: fast and _____

When and Why I Listen to It	• on the bus in the morning
	  - makes me _____
	  - listen to it until I _____
	• when I exercise, I _____ my favorite songs
	  - help me _____ after a long day

52

C **Complete the paragraph by using the model text.**

I Like Pop Music Best

Introduction

How I Learned About It

I like many types of music, but my favorite genre is _____.

I learned about _____ from my _____.

Body

About the Genre

_____ is _____ by _____.

There _____. The songs

When and Why I Listen to It

are _____. I _____ listen to

_____. The music makes me

_____. I _____.

When I _____, I _____.

They help me _____.

Conclusion

If you like _____ music, why don't you _____?

Collecting Ideas

Look at the example. Fill in the blanks with the phrases in the box.

beautiful and relaxing ~~fast and upbeat~~ stay happy all day
loud and fast improve my dance skills smooth and relaxing

1

- pop
- _fast and upbeat_
- help me relieve stress after a long day

2

- classical
- _____
- help me focus on studying

3

- rock
- _____
- help me forget my worries

4

- hip hop
- fast and upbeat
- help me _____

5

- jazz
- _____
- help me relax after a long week

6

- dance
- fast and energetic
- help me _____

54

Sentence Practice

Ⓐ Look at the example and complete the sentences.

pop music / a singer or a group
→ Pop music **is performed by** a singer or a group.

🎙 Use the passive "be + p.p. + by" to focus on the person or thing that is affected by an action.

1 jazz / a small band

→ _____

2 rock music / a band

→ _____

3 hip hop / a singer or a rapper

→ _____

4 classical music / a small group or an orchestra

→ _____

Your Idea

5 _____

Ⓑ Look at the example and complete the sentences.

1 (fast / upbeat)

→ **The songs are usually** fast **and** upbeat. _____

2 (beautiful / relaxing)

→ _____

3 (loud / fast)

→ _____

4 (fast / energetic)

→ _____

Your Idea

5 _____

C Look at the pictures. Complete the sentences with the phrases in the box.

do my homework	~~exercise after school~~	go to dance class

1 _____When I_ exercise after school ___, I dance to my favorite songs.

2 _____, I listen to my favorite songs.

3 _____, I put on my favorite songs.

D Look at the example and complete the sentences.

1 (relieve stress after a long day)

→ **They help me** relieve stress after a long day. _____

2 (focus on studying)

→ _____

3 (improve my dance skills)

→ _____

E Look at the example and rewrite the sentences.

💡 Use "why don't you ~?" to make a recommendation.

1 You like cheerful music. You should listen to pop.

→ **If** you like cheerful music, **why don't you** listen to pop**?** ___

2 You like relaxing music. You should listen to classical.

→ _____

3 You like upbeat music. You should listen to hip hop.

→ _____

Sentence Practice Plus

A **Read the short paragraph. Correct the mistakes and rewrite the sentences.**

 Rock music is <u>perform</u> by a band. The songs are usually loud <u>but</u> fast. <u>Where</u> my friends come over, I put on my favorite album. If you like energetic music, why <u>do</u> you listen to rock?

_____

_____

_____

_____

B **Look at the picture and read the conditions. Write about hip hop like A above.**

Conditions

① Write four sentences.

② Include the following information: a singer or a rapper / fast, upbeat / go to dance class – put on my favorite songs / upbeat music.

③ Include "be + p.p. + by" and "If you ~, why don't you ~?"

_____

_____

_____

_____

Brainstorming

Write about your favorite musical genre. Complete the graphic organizer. Use the ideas in Collecting Ideas or come up with your own.

I Like _____ Best	
How I Learned About It	
About the Genre	• • •
When and Why I Listen to It	• — — • —

◆ More Musical Genres

opera / rhythm and blues (R&B) / techno / K-pop / country / disco / punk rock

First Draft

Complete the first draft by using the graphic organizer.

Title _____

Introduction

How I Learned About It

I like many types of music, but my favorite genre is _____.

I learned about _____ from _____.

Body

About the Genre

_____ is _____ by _____.

_____. There _____.

When and Why I Listen to It

The songs are _____. I _____

listen to _____.

The music makes me _____.

I _____.

When _____, I _____

_____. They help me _____.

Conclusion

If you like _____ music, why don't you _____

_____?

Unit 6

My Favorite Holiday

Writing Goal	Write about your favorite holiday.
Type of Writing	Expository Writing » Email
	Expository writing gives information about a topic or tells you how to do something.

Before You Write

A **Read and answer the questions.**

1 What is your favorite holiday?

My favorite holiday is _____.

2 Where do you go on your favorite holiday?

I go to _____.

3 What do you do on your favorite holiday?

I _____.

B **Match the pictures with the holidays in the box.**

> Christmas   Children's Day   Thanksgiving
> Lunar New Year   Valentine's Day   Independence Day

1

_____

2

_____

3

_____

4

_____

5

_____

6

_____

Understanding the Model Text

A **Read the model text and answer the question.**

To : Irina000@mail.com
Subject : **Thanksgiving**

Dear Irina,

What is your favorite holiday? Mine is Thanksgiving! Thanksgiving is celebrated in the U.S., Canada, and the U.K. In the U.S., it is on the fourth Thursday in November. We usually eat turkey and pumpkin pie on this day. Every year, my family goes to my aunt's house. Everyone brings some food, such as mashed potatoes or stuffing. I set the table and help my aunt make the pumpkin pie. Baking the pie is so much fun. Then we eat and talk about the things that we are thankful for. This year, I am thankful for my friends and family. I hope we celebrate Thanksgiving together for many more years!

Your friend,

James

Q What is the passage mainly about?

a. James' favorite holiday

b. what Irina does on Thanksgiving

B **Read the model text again and complete the graphic organizer.**

Thanksgiving	
Where and When	• _____ in the U.S., Canada, and the U.K. • _____ in November
What We Do	eat turkey and _____
What My Family Does	• family – goes to _____ • I – set the table and _____ make the pumpkin pie • we – eat and talk about the things that we _____

C Complete the paragraph by using the model text.

Title	My Favorite Holiday: Thanksgiving

Introduction

Dear _____,

What is your favorite holiday? Mine is _____!

Body

Where and When

_____ is celebrated in _____.

In _____, it is on _____

What We Do

in _____. We usually _____

What My Family Does

on this day. Every year, _____.

Everyone _____.

I _____ and _____.

_____ is _____. Then we _____

_____.

This year, I _____.

Conclusion

I hope we celebrate _____ together for many more years!

Your friend,

_____

Collecting Ideas

Look at the example. Fill in the blanks with the phrases in the box.

sing Christmas songs	~~turkey and pumpkin pie~~	spend time with our families
watch the fireworks	give chocolate and candy	rice cake soup and dumplings

1

- Thanksgiving
- the U.S.: fourth Thursday in November
- eat ___turkey and pumpkin pie___

2

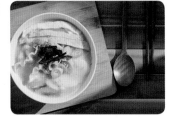

- Lunar New Year
- Korea: first day of the lunar calendar
- eat _____

3

- Christmas
- Canada: the 25th of December
- exchange gifts and

  _____

4

- Valentine's Day
- Australia: the 14th of February
- _____

  to our friends

5

- Independence Day
- the U.S.: the 4th of July
- have a barbecue and

  _____

6

- Children's Day
- China: the first day of June
- have a picnic and

  _____

Sentence Practice

A Look at the example and complete the sentences.

> the U.S. / the fourth Thursday in November
> → **In** the U.S., **it is on** the fourth Thursday in November.

1 Korea / the first day of the lunar calendar

→ _____

2 Canada / the 25th of December

→ _____

3 Australia / the 14th of February

→ _____

4 China / the first day of June

→ _____

Your Idea

5 _____

B Look at the pictures. Complete the sentences with the phrases in the box.

> eat rice cake soup / dumplings   have a barbecue / watch the fireworks
> ~~eat turkey / pumpkin pie~~   exchange gifts / sing Christmas songs

1 **We usually** eat turkey **and** pumpkin pie. _____

2 _____

3 _____

4 _____

C Look at the example and rewrite the sentences.

1 I bake the pie. It is so much fun.

→ **Baking** the pie is so much fun.

2 I cook the dumplings. It is so much fun.

→ _____

3 I decorate the tree. It is so exciting.

→ _____

D Look at the example and rewrite the sentences.

💡 Use the relative pronoun "that" to combine two related sentences.

1 We eat and talk about the things. We are thankful for the things.

→ We eat and talk about the things **that** we are thankful for.

2 We bow to our elders and eat the food. My grandma made the food.

→ _____

3 We go to the park and fly the kite. We bought the kite.

→ _____

E Look at the example and complete the sentences.

💡 Use the preposition "for" before a noun and "to" before a verb.

1 (thankful / my friends and family)

→ **This year, I am** thankful **for** my friends and family.

2 (excited / eat some rice cakes)

→ _____

3 (eager / open my presents)

→ _____

Sentence Practice Plus

A **Read the short paragraph. Correct the mistakes and rewrite the sentences.**

In Canada, Christmas is <u>in</u> the 25th of December. I wrap some presents and <u>helps</u> my brother decorate the tree. <u>Decorate</u> the tree is so exciting. Then we eat and exchange the gifts <u>who</u> we wrapped.

_____

_____

_____

_____

B **Look at the picture and read the conditions. Write about Children's Day in China like A above.**

Conditions

① Write four sentences.

② Include the following information: the first day of June / go to the shopping mall – my sister, choose a kite / pick out the kite / go to the park – fly the kite.

③ Include "verb-ing" as a subject and the relative pronoun "that."

_____

_____

_____

_____

Brainstorming

Write about your favorite holiday. Complete the graphic organizer. Use the ideas in Collecting Ideas or come up with your own.

My Favorite Holiday: _____	
Where and When	• •
What We Do	
What My Family Does	• • •

● **More Holidays**

Easter / Parents' Day / Halloween / Diwali / Hanukkah / New Year's Eve / Buddha's Birthday

First Draft

Complete the first draft by using the graphic organizer.

Title _____

Introduction

Dear _____,

What is your favorite holiday? Mine is _____!

Body

Where and When

_____ is celebrated in _____

_____. In _____, it is on _____

What We Do

_____. We _____

_____ on this day. Every year,

What My Family Does

_____.

Everyone _____.

_____.

_____ is _____. Then we

_____.

This year, I _____.

Conclusion

I hope we celebrate _____ together for many

more years!

Your friend,

_____

Unit 7

Volunteering

Writing Goal	Write about volunteering.
Type of Writing	Narrative Writing 〉 Report

Narrative writing describes a story that happened to you. Narrative writing can also describe imaginary events.

Before You Write

A **Read and answer the questions.**

1 Do you like to volunteer?

☐ Yes, I do. ☐ No, I don't.

2 Where did you volunteer?

I volunteered at a(n) _____.

3 Where do you want to volunteer in the future?

I want to volunteer at a(n) _____.

B **Fill in the chart with the words and phrases in the box.**

residents   soup kitchen   children's hospital   sick children
animal shelter   homeless people   nursing home   animals

Places to Volunteer	Those in Need
• _____	• _____
• _____	• _____
• _____	• _____
• _____	• _____

Understanding the Model Text

A Read the model text and answer the question.

Volunteering at the Children's Hospital

Last year, I decided to do some volunteer work. First, I thought about places to volunteer at. I chose the children's hospital near my house. There are many sick children there. They can't play or go to school. That made me feel very sad. Every Saturday, I went to the hospital at 1:00 P.M. I played board games with the children and read them books. They were so happy to play with me. I went home at 5:00 P.M. I always felt much happier after spending time with them. Although I am young, I'm glad that I can help the children. I am going to volunteer there again this year.

Q The topic sentence is the main idea of the passage. Underline the topic sentence.

B Read the model text again and complete the graphic organizer.

At the Children's Hospital	
Who Was There	many _____ → can't play or go to school
How I Felt Before	made me feel _____
What I Did	• every Saturday → went to _____ at 1:00 P.M. • played _____ with the children • read them books → they were so happy to _____ • _____ at 5:00 P.M.
How I Felt After	• _____ after spending time with them • glad that I can _____

C **Complete the paragraph by using the model text.**

Title	Volunteering at the Children's Hospital

Introduction

Last year, I decided to do some _____. First, I

thought about places _____.

Body

I chose _____ near my house. There are

Who Was There _____ there. They _____

How I Felt Before _____. That made me feel _____.

What I Did _____, I went to _____ at

_____. I _____

_____. They _____.

How I Felt After I went home at _____. I always felt _____

after _____.

Conclusion

_____ I am _____, I'm glad that _____

_____. I am going to volunteer there _____

_____.

Collecting Ideas

Look at the example. Fill in the blanks with the phrases in the box.

talk with them   ~~read them books~~   prepare lunch for the homeless
teach the children   do art with the children   clean the cages

1

- Children's hospital
- play board games with the children
  and _____read them books_____

2

- Nursing home
- play games with the residents and
  _____

3

- Animal shelter
- _____
  and walk the dogs

4

- Soup kitchen
- _____
  and serve it to them

5

- Community center
- _____
  and play games with them

6

- Orphanage
- _____
  math and English

Sentence Practice

A **Look at the pictures and complete the sentences.**

have homes / families   live on the streets / in shelters
go outside / see their families often   ~~play / go to school~~

1 They can't _____ play **or** go to school _____ .

2 They _____ .

3 They can't _____ .

4 They don't _____ .

B **Look at the example and complete the sentences.**

Saturday / hospital / 1:00 P.M.
→ **Every** Saturday, **I went to the** hospital **at** 1:00 P.M.

1 Sunday / nursing home / 10:00 A.M.

→ _____

2 Wednesday / orphanage / 3:00 P.M.

→ _____

3 Saturday / soup kitchen / 9:00 A.M.

→ _____

4 Monday / animal shelter / 4:00 P.M.

→ _____

Your Idea

5 _____

C Look at the example and complete the sentences.

1 play board games with the children / read them books

→ **I played** board games with the children **and read** them books. _____

2 play games with the residents / talk with them

→ _____

3 clean the cages / walk the dogs

→ _____

D Look at the example and complete the sentences.

💡 Use "much" and the comparative form of the adjective to explain a large change.

1 (happy / spend time with them)

→ **I always felt much happier after spending** time with them. _____

2 (good / spend time with them)

→ _____

3 (calm / teach the children)

→ _____

E Look at the example and rewrite the sentences.

💡 Use "although" to contrast two ideas.

1 I am young, but I'm glad that I can help the children.

→ **Although** I am young, I'm glad that I can help the children. _____

2 I am a teenager, but I'm glad that I can help the residents.

→ _____

3 I am not a teacher, but I'm glad that I can teach the children.

→ _____

Sentence Practice Plus

A **Read the short paragraph. Correct the mistakes and rewrite the sentences.**

Every Saturday, I went to the soup kitchen in 9:00 A.M. I prepare lunch for the homeless and served it to them. I always felt much good after serving the food. But I am not a chef, I'm glad that I can serve the homeless.

_____

_____

_____

_____

B **Look at the picture and read the conditions. Write about the animal shelter like A above.**

Conditions

① Write four sentences.

② Include the following information: Monday – 4:00 P.M. / clean the cages – walk the dogs / feel happy / not an adult – help the animals.

③ Include "much + comparative adjective" and "although."

_____

_____

_____

_____

Brainstorming

Write about volunteering. Complete the graphic organizer. Use the ideas in Collecting Ideas or come up with your own.

Volunteering at the _____	
Who Was There	
How I Felt Before	
What I Did	• • • ⟶ •
How I Felt After	• •

☛ **More Places to Volunteer**

a public library / a wildlife preserve / a summer camp / a charity car wash / a park clean-up

First Draft

Complete the first draft by using the graphic organizer.

Title _____

Introduction _____, I decided to do some _____.

First, I thought about places _____.

Body

I chose _____. There are

Who Was There _____ there. They _____

How I Felt Before _____. That made me _____

What I Did _____ . _____, I went to _____

_____ at _____ . I _____

_____ .

They _____. I went home

How I Felt After at _____. I always felt _____ after

_____ .

Conclusion

Although _____, I'm glad that I

_____. I am going to volunteer there

again _____ .

Unit 8

My Book Report

Writing Goal	Write about a book you read.
Type of Writing	Expository Writing » Book Report

Expository writing gives information about a topic or tells you how to do something.

Before You Write

A **Read and answer the questions.**

1 Do you like to read books?

☐ Yes, I do. ☐ No, I don't.

2 What is your favorite book?

My favorite book is _____ .

3 Who is the main character of the book?

The main character is _____ .

B **Fill in the chart with the words in the box.**

brave	queen	clever	prince
cute	orphan	interesting	pilot

Characters	Adjectives
• _____	• _____
• _____	• _____
• _____	• _____
• _____	• _____

Understanding the Model Text

A Read the model text and answer the question.

A Book Report: *Alice's Adventures in Wonderland*

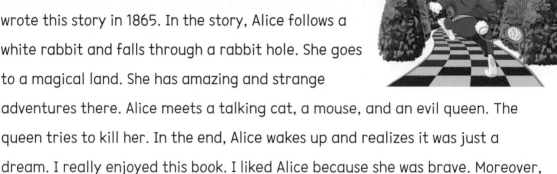

My favorite book is *Alice's Adventures in Wonderland*. It is about a young girl named Alice. Lewis Carroll wrote this story in 1865. In the story, Alice follows a white rabbit and falls through a rabbit hole. She goes to a magical land. She has amazing and strange adventures there. Alice meets a talking cat, a mouse, and an evil queen. The queen tries to kill her. In the end, Alice wakes up and realizes it was just a dream. I really enjoyed this book. I liked Alice because she was brave. Moreover, the story was very fun to read. I think everyone should read this book.

Q What is the passage mainly about?
   a. a story about a girl named Alice
   b. Lewis Carroll's books

B Read the model text again and complete the graphic organizer.

Alice's Adventures in Wonderland	
The Author	_____ wrote this story in _____
The Plot	• The main character – a young girl _____ • Alice follows _____ and falls through a rabbit hole • goes to _____ • has amazing and _____ there • meets a talking cat, a mouse, and _____ • queen tries to _____ • In the end: Alice wakes up and realizes it was just _____
My Opinion	• liked Alice because she was _____ • story was _____

C **Complete the paragraph by using the model text.**

| Title | A Book Report: *Alice's Adventures in Wonderland* |

Introduction

The Main Character

My favorite book is _____.

It is about _____ named _____.

The Author

_____ wrote this story in _____.

Body

The Plot

In the story, _____

_____. _____.

_____.

_____.

_____. In the end, _____

_____. I really enjoyed this book.

My Opinion

I liked _____ because _____. Moreover,

the story was very _____ to read.

Conclusion

I think everyone _____ this book.

Collecting Ideas

Look at the example. Fill in the blanks with the phrases in the box.

wins an award	goes to school	~~a magical land~~
takes care of her family	gets into trouble	meets a little prince

1

Alice's Adventures in Wonderland

- Alice:
- goes to ___a magical land___
- wakes up and realizes it was just a dream

2

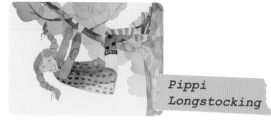

Pippi Longstocking

- Pippi:
- is very naughty and

  _____ a lot
- rescues some children and becomes a hero

3

Anne of Green Gables

- Anne:
- is smart but doesn't fit in at school
- becomes a teacher and

  _____

4

Wonder

- Auggie:
- is scared but goes to school for the first time
- _____ for bravery

5

The Little Prince

- A Pilot:
- _____ with golden hair
- the little prince goes home

6

Matilda

- Matilda:
- wants to learn, so she

  _____
- goes to live with Miss Honey

Sentence Practice

A **Look at the example and rewrite the sentences.**

> It is about a young girl. Her name is Alice.
> → It is about a young girl **named** Alice.

🔦 Use a "past participle phrase" to modify a noun.

1 It is about a funny girl. Her name is Pippi.

➡ _____

2 It is about a young boy. His name is Auggie.

➡ _____

3 It is about a special girl. Her name is Matilda.

➡ _____

Your Idea

4 _____

B **Read the plot of *Anne of Green Gables* and write the phrases.**

> fit in   she meets   becomes a teacher
> live on a farm   grows up   orphan girl

1 In the story, Anne is a lonely _____ .

2 She goes to _____ in Avonlea.

3 Anne is smart but doesn't _____ at school.

4 _____ a girl named Diana and a boy named Gilbert.

5 Anne _____ and wants to become a teacher.

6 In the end, Anne _____ and takes care of her family.

C Read the plot of *The Little Prince* and write the sentences.

> In the end, the little prince goes home.
> He meets a little prince with golden hair.
> He traveled to many planets and met many people.

1 In the story, the pilot crashes his plane in the desert.

2 _____

3 The prince explains that he came from another planet.

4 _____

5 The pilot is very thirsty, so they look for water together.

6 _____

D Look at the example and rewrite the sentences.

Use "adjective + to-infinitive" to express feelings.

1 I read the story. It was very fun.

→ **The story** was very fun **to read**.

2 I read the story. It was very exciting.

→ _____

3 I read the story. It was very heartwarming.

→ _____

4 I read the story. It was very entertaining.

→ _____

Sentence Practice Plus

A **Read the short paragraph. Correct the mistakes and rewrite the sentences.**

My favorite <u>books</u> is *Matilda*. It is about a special girl <u>name</u> Matilda. I liked Matilda <u>but</u> she was so clever. Moreover, the story was very fun to <u>reading</u>.

_____

_____

_____

_____

B **Look at the picture and read the conditions. Write about *Wonder* like A above.**

Conditions

① Write four sentences.

② Include the following information: *Wonder* / young boy – Auggie / very kind / story – very entertaining.

③ Include a past participle and "adjective + to-infinitive."

_____

_____

_____

_____

Brainstorming

Write about a book you read. Complete the graphic organizer. Use the ideas in Collecting Ideas or come up with your own.

A Book Report: _____	
The Author	
The Plot	• • • • • • • In the end:
My Opinion	• •

• **More Books**

A Christmas Carol – Charles Dickens / *James and the Giant Peach* – Roald Dahl / *Charlotte's Web* – E.B. White / *The Lion, the Witch, and the Wardrobe* – C.S. Lewis

First Draft

Complete the first draft by using the graphic organizer.

Title _____

Introduction

The Main Character

My favorite book is _____ .

It is about _____ named _____ .

The Author

_____ wrote this story in _____ .

Body

The Plot

In the story, _____ .

_____ .

_____ .

_____ .

_____ .

In the end, _____ .

My Opinion

I really enjoyed this book. I liked _____ because

_____ . Moreover, the story was

_____ to read.

Conclusion

I think everyone _____ this book.

Vocabulary & Structure Review

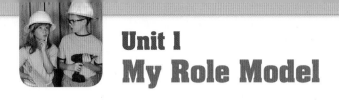

Unit 1
My Role Model

Words & Phrases

Read the words and phrases. Write the meaning next to each word and phrase.

1	role model		11	successful	
2	businessman		12	gold medalist	
3	actress (*cf.* actor)		13	president	
4	activist		14	win (won-won)	
5	nun		15	athlete	
6	lawyer		16	championship	
7	found (founded-founded)		17	racism	
8	popular		18	impress	
9	billionaire		19	star (*v.*)	
10	charity		20	donate	

Structures

1 relative pronoun "who"

e.g He is a businessman who founded Microsoft.

2 as a result

e.g As a result, Bill Gates became a billionaire at age 31.

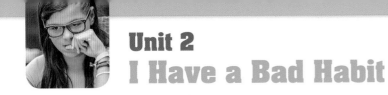

Unit 2
I Have a Bad Habit

Words & Phrases

Read the words and phrases. Write the meaning next to each word and phrase.

1	habit		11	restless	
2	bite		12	nervous	
3	nail		13	stress out	
4	terrible (= bad)		14	take a deep breath	
5	remind		15	these days	
6	practice (v.)		16	set a timer	
7	healthy		17	tie one's hair back	
8	calm (a., v.)		18	stay up late	
9	relaxed		19	put on	
10	tap		20	break a habit	

Structures

1 simple future tense "will"

e.g I <u>will</u> put tape around my fingers.

This <u>will</u> remind me to stop biting my nails.

2 instead of + verb-ing

e.g <u>Instead of</u> biting my nails, I will take deep breaths.

Unit 3
A Restaurant Review

Read the words and phrases. Write the meaning next to each word and phrase.

1	review (*n.*)		11	spicy	
2	order (*v.*)		12	oily	
3	amazing		13	juicy	
4	fresh		14	delicious	
5	creamy		15	bland	
6	fluffy		16	bitter	
7	service		17	crunchy	
8	unfortunately (↔ fortunately)		18	rude	
9	recommend		19	manager	
10	loud		20	comfortable (↔ uncomfortable)	

Structures

1 both *A* and *B*

e.g <u>Both</u> the steak <u>and</u> the cream pasta tasted amazing.

2 make + object + verb

e.g The waiter <u>made us laugh</u>.

94

Unit 4
I Have a Problem

Read the words and phrases. Write the meaning next to each word and phrase.

1	shy		11	follow	
2	solve		12	acne	
3	cure (v.)		13	reduce	
4	memorize		14	clumsy (n. clumsiness)	
5	clearly		15	pack (v.)	
6	in front of		16	do a presentation	
7	crowd		17	get worse	
8	cause (v.)		18	pay attention	
9	advice		19	slippery surface	
10	tip		20	wear makeup	

Structures

1 how to + verb

e.g Please tell me <u>how to solve</u> this!

2 had better + verb

e.g If your shyness gets worse, you <u>had better talk</u> to someone.

Unit 5
My Favorite Musical Genre

Read the words and phrases. Write the meaning next to each word and phrase.

1	genre		11	improve	
2	pop music		12	until	
3	classical		13	exercise	
4	learn		14	relieve	
5	perform		15	stay	
6	upbeat		16	band	
7	cheerful		17	get to	
8	smooth		18	focus on	
9	relax (*cf.* relaxing)		19	all day	
10	energetic		20	come over	

Structures

1 passive: be + p.p. + by

e.g Pop music <u>is performed by</u> a singer or a group.

2 If you ~, why don't you + verb ~?

e.g <u>If you</u> like cheerful music, <u>why don't you listen</u> to pop?

Unit 6
My Favorite Holiday

Read the words and phrases. Write the meaning next to each word and phrase.

1	holiday		11	firework	
2	celebrate		12	decorate	
3	mashed potatoes		13	bow	
4	stuffing		14	elder (*n.*)	
5	bake		15	eager	
6	Thanksgiving		16	wrap	
7	Lunar New Year		17	set the table	
8	Independence Day		18	be thankful for	
9	dumpling		19	fly a kite	
10	exchange		20	pick out	

Structures

1 gerund (verb-ing) as a subject

e.g Baking the pie is so much fun.

2 "that" as the object of a relative clause

e.g We eat and talk about the things that we are thankful for.

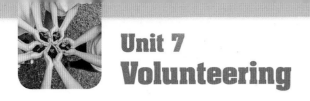

Unit 7
Volunteering

Read the words and phrases. Write the meaning next to each word and phrase.

1	volunteer (v.)		11	orphanage	
2	volunteer work		12	chef	
3	glad		13	adult	
4	resident		14	nursing home	
5	clean (v.)		15	animal shelter	
6	cage		16	soup kitchen	
7	street		17	community center	
8	homeless		18	play board games	
9	serve (v.)		19	walk the dog	
10	prepare		20	spend time with	

Structures

1 much + comparative adjective

e.g I always felt <u>much happier</u> after spending time with them.

2 although + subject + verb

e.g <u>Although I am young</u>, I'm glad that I can help the children.

Unit 8
My Book Report

Read the words and phrases. Write the meaning next to each word and phrase.

1	name (v.)		11	thirsty	
2	magical		12	crash (v.)	
3	adventure		13	explain	
4	evil (a.)		14	planet	
5	realize		15	heartwarming	
6	brave		16	entertaining	
7	bravery		17	in the end	
8	naughty		18	get into trouble	
9	rescue		19	fit in	
10	hero		20	win an award	

Structures

1 past participle

e.g It is about a young girl <u>named</u> Alice.

2 adjective + to-infinitive

e.g The story was very <u>fun to read</u>.

Memo

Memo

Memo

Memo

Memo

Essential Guide to Writing
Writing Avenue

Workbook

Paragraph Writing

3

Essential Guide to Writing

Writing Avenue

Workbook

Paragraph Writing

3

DARAKWON

Unit 1 My Role Model

Ⓐ Look at the example and complete the sentences.

1 (he / a businessman) (founded Microsoft)

   → He **is** a businessman **who** founded Microsoft. _____

2 (she / a figure skater) (won many medals)

   → _____

3 (he / a soccer player) (won many championships)

   → _____

4 (she / an actress) (starred in many movies)

   → _____

Ⓑ Look at the example and complete the sentences. Change the tense to past tense.

1 (Bill Gates / become a billionaire at age 31)

   → **As a result,** Bill Gates **became** a billionaire at age 31. _____

2 (Mother Teresa / decide to found a charity)

   → _____

3 (Nelson Mandela / win the Nobel Peace Prize in 1993)

   → _____

4 (Angelina Jolie / become one of the most famous actresses)

   → _____

C **Match the phrases. Then, write the sentences.**

1	He made our lives	•	• very popular
2	Bill Gates was born	•	• him in the future
3	He wanted people to	•	• in the U.S. in 1955
4	He spent a lot of time	•	• and help many people
5	His computers became	•	• building his company
6	I want to be successful	•	• better and easier
7	I hope that I can be like	•	• helped people in poor countries
8	He also started a charity and	•	• have their own computers at home

1 _____

2 _____

3 _____

4 _____

5 _____

6 _____

7 _____

8 _____

Revise & Edit

Write about your role model. Refer to the First Draft in the student book. Then, edit your paragraph.

Title

Introduction

Body

Conclusion

Editing Checklist ☐ Capitalization ☐ Punctuation ☐ Grammar ☐ Spelling

Final Draft

Write the final draft.

Title

Unit 2 I Have a Bad Habit

A **Look at the example and complete the sentences.**

1 remind me to stop biting my nails

→ **This will** remind me to stop biting my nails. _____

2 fill me up and keep me healthy

→ _____

3 make me feel sleepy and relaxed

→ _____

4 use up my extra energy

→ _____

B **Look at the example and complete the sentences.**

1 bite my nails / take deep breaths

→ **Instead of biting** my nails, **I will** take deep breaths. _____

2 tap my feet / stand up and stretch

→ _____

3 watch TV / close my eyes and breathe deeply

→ _____

4 play for hours / use my phone for thirty minutes

→ _____

C **Match the phrases. Then, write the sentences.**

1 First, I will put tape ·   · my nails

2 Then I will feel calm ·   · and relaxed

3 When I feel stressed, ·   · healthy habits

4 These days, I always bite ·   · I was stressed out

5 I started doing this because ·   · around my fingers

6 Second, I will practice some ·   · break my bad habit

7 My teacher said I should stop ·   · I will bite the tape instead

8 It won't be easy, but I am sure I can · · doing it, so I made a plan

1 _____

2 _____

3 _____

4 _____

5 _____

6 _____

7 _____

8 _____

Revise & Edit

Write about your bad habit. Refer to the First Draft in the student book. Then, edit your paragraph.

Title	

Introduction

Body

Conclusion

Editing Checklist ☐ Capitalization ☐ Punctuation ☐ Grammar ☐ Spelling

Final Draft

Write the final draft.

Title

Unit 3 A Restaurant Review

Ⓐ Look at the example and complete the sentences.

1 | steak / cream pasta / amazing |

→ **Both the** steak **and the** cream pasta **tasted** amazing.

2 | sushi rolls / noodles / great |

→ _____

3 | beef tacos / chicken burritos / delicious |

→ _____

4 | hamburgers / French fries / wonderful |

→ _____

Ⓑ Look at the example and rewrite the sentences.

1 We laughed because of him.

→ **He made us laugh.**

2 We waited for a long time because of him.

→ _____

3 We smiled because of her.

→ _____

4 We tried the food because of her.

→ _____

C **Match the phrases. Then, write the sentences.**

1. The cake was •
2. I thought •
3. For dessert, •
4. Unfortunately, the restaurant •
5. The salad was very small •
6. I ate at Teddy's Grill House •
7. All in all, Teddy's Grill House is •
8. Both the steak •

- • was very noisy
- • sweet and fluffy
- • and expensive
- • we had chocolate cake
- • the waiter was funny
- • a great place to eat
- • last week with my mom
- • and the cream pasta tasted amazing

1 _____

2 _____

3 _____

4 _____

5 _____

6 _____

7 _____

8 _____

Revise & Edit

Write a review of a restaurant you went to. Refer to the First Draft in the student book. Then, edit your paragraph.

Title	

Introduction

Body

Conclusion

Editing Checklist ☐ Capitalization ☐ Punctuation ☐ Grammar ☐ Spelling

Final Draft

Write the final draft.

Title	

Unit 4 I Have a Problem

A Look at the example and rewrite the sentences.

1 | I need to solve this. Can you tell me how? |

→ **Please tell me how to solve this!**

2 | I need to fix this. Can you tell me how? |

→ _____

3 | I need to cure this. Can you tell me how? |

→ _____

4 | I need to make friends. Can you tell me how? |

→ _____

B Look at the example and rewrite the sentences.

1 Your shyness gets worse. You should talk to someone.

→ **If** your shyness gets worse, you **had better** talk to someone. _____

2 Your acne gets worse. You should see a doctor.

→ _____

3 Your clumsiness gets worse. You should try yoga.

→ _____

4 Your problem gets worse. You should talk to your teacher.

→ _____

C **Match the phrases. Then, write the sentences.**

1	You must feel	•	•	a few tips
2	Here are	•	•	from your teacher
3	Memorize the words	•	•	bad about being shy
4	You can get advice	•	•	in front of a crowd
5	This can cause stress,	•	•	and speak clearly
6	Follow these tips,	•	•	I'm too shy
7	I have to do a presentation, but	•	•	and you will be less shy
8	Second, many people feel nervous	•	•	so try to breathe deeply

1 _____

2 _____

3 _____

4 _____

5 _____

6 _____

7 _____

8 _____

Revise & Edit

Write about how to solve a problem. Refer to the First Draft in the student book. Then, edit your paragraph.

Title

Introduction

Body

Conclusion

Editing Checklist ☐ Capitalization ☐ Punctuation ☐ Grammar ☐ Spelling

Final Draft

Write the final draft.

Title

Unit 5 My Favorite Musical Genre

Ⓐ **Look at the example and complete the sentences.**

1 | pop music / perform / a singer or a group |

→ Pop music **is performed by** a singer or a group.
_____

2 | dance music / perform / a DJ or a singer |

→ _____

3 | hip hop / perform / a singer or a rapper |

→ _____

4 | jazz / perform / a small band |

→ _____

Ⓑ **Look at the example and rewrite the sentences.**

1 You like cheerful music, so listen to pop.

→ **If** you like cheerful music, **why don't you** listen to pop?
_____

2 You like energetic music, so listen to rock.

→ _____

3 You like relaxing music, so listen to jazz.

→ _____

4 You like exciting music, so listen to dance.

→ _____

C **Match the phrases. Then, write the sentences.**

1 I listen to it until	•	• and upbeat
2 I learned about pop music	•	• from my sister
3 There are singers	•	• I get to school
4 The songs are usually fast	•	• my favorite genre is pop
5 They help me relieve	•	• on the bus in the morning
6 I always listen to pop music	•	• I dance to my favorite songs
7 When I exercise after school,	•	• and dancers in the group
8 I like many types of music, but	•	• stress after a long day

1 _____

2 _____

3 _____

4 _____

5 _____

6 _____

7 _____

8 _____

Revise & Edit

Write about your favorite musical genre. Refer to the First Draft in the student book. Then, edit your paragraph.

Title	

Introduction	

Body	

Conclusion	

Editing Checklist ☐ Capitalization ☐ Punctuation ☐ Grammar ☐ Spelling

Final Draft

Write the final draft.

Title

Unit 6 My Favorite Holiday

A **Look at the example and complete the sentences.**

1 bake / pie / so much fun

→ **Baking the** pie **is** so much fun. _____

2 cook / dumplings / so much fun

→ _____

3 make / chocolates / very difficult

→ _____

4 fly / kite / so exciting

→ _____

B **Look at the example and complete the sentences.**

1 talk about the things / we are thankful for

→ **We** talk about the things **that** we are thankful for. _____

2 give away the delicious treats / we made

→ _____

3 light the fireworks / we bought

→ _____

4 exchange the gifts / we wrapped

→ _____

22

C **Match the phrases. Then, write the sentences.**

1	Every year, my family goes	•	• my friends and family
2	Thanksgiving is celebrated	•	• to my aunt's house
3	In the U.S., it is on	•	• my aunt make the pumpkin pie
4	We usually eat turkey	•	• together for many more years
5	This year, I am thankful for	•	• and pumpkin pie on this day
6	I set the table and help	•	• such as mashed potatoes or stuffing
7	Everyone brings some food,	•	• the fourth Thursday in November
8	I hope we celebrate Thanksgiving	•	• in the U.S., Canada, and the U.K.

1 _____

2 _____

3 _____

4 _____

5 _____

6 _____

7 _____

8 _____

Revise & Edit

Write about your favorite holiday. Refer to the First Draft in the student book. Then, edit your paragraph.

Title

Introduction

Body

Conclusion

Final Draft

Write the final draft.

Title

Unit 7 Volunteering

A **Look at the example and rewrite the sentences.**

1 | I always felt happy after spending time with them. |

→ I always felt **much happier** after spending time with them.

2 | I always felt good after helping the animals. |

→ _____

3 | I always felt calm after teaching the children. |

→ _____

4 | I always felt happy after serving the food. |

→ _____

B **Look at the example and rewrite the sentences.**

1 I am young. I'm glad that I can help the children.

→ **Although** I am young, I'm glad that I can help the children.

2 I am a teenager. I'm glad that I can help the residents.

→ _____

3 I am not a chef. I'm glad that I can serve the homeless.

→ _____

4 I am not a teacher. I'm glad that I can teach the children.

→ _____

C **Match the phrases. Then, write the sentences.**

1	That made me	•	• near my house
2	They were so happy	•	• feel very sad
3	I am going to volunteer	•	• to play with me
4	Every Saturday, I went	•	• places to volunteer at
5	I chose the children's hospital	•	• do some volunteer work
6	Last year, I decided to	•	• there again this year
7	First, I thought about	•	• to the hospital at 1:00 P.M.
8	I played board games with	•	• the children and read them books

1 _____

2 _____

3 _____

4 _____

5 _____

6 _____

7 _____

8 _____

Revise & Edit

Write about volunteering. Refer to the First Draft in the student book. Then, edit your paragraph.

Title

Introduction

Body

Conclusion

Editing Checklist ☐ Capitalization ☐ Punctuation ☐ Grammar ☐ Spelling

Final Draft

Write the final draft.

Title

Unit 8 My Book Report

A **Look at the example and rewrite the sentences.**

1 It is about Alice. (young girl)

→ It is about **a** young girl **named** Alice. _____

2 It is about Pippi. (funny girl)

→ _____

3 It is about Auggie. (young boy)

→ _____

4 It is about Matilda. (special girl)

→ _____

B **Look at the example and complete the sentences.**

1 (the story / fun)

→ The story **was very** fun **to read**. _____

2 (the story / heartwarming)

→ _____

3 (the story / entertaining)

→ _____

4 (the story / interesting)

→ _____

C **Match the phrases. Then, write the sentences.**

1	Lewis Carroll wrote	•	• to kill her
2	I liked Alice because	•	• read this book
3	I think everyone should	•	• she was brave
4	The queen tries	•	• this story in 1865
5	Alice meets a talking cat,	•	• strange adventures there
6	In the end, Alice wakes up	•	• a mouse, and an evil queen
7	She has amazing and	•	• falls through a rabbit hole
8	In the story, Alice follows a white rabbit and	•	• and realizes it was just a dream

1 _____

2 _____

3 _____

4 _____

5 _____

6 _____

7 _____

8 _____

Revise & Edit

Write about a book you read. Refer to the First Draft in the student book. Then, edit your paragraph.

Title

Introduction

Body

Conclusion

Editing Checklist   ☐ Capitalization   ☐ Punctuation   ☐ Grammar   ☐ Spelling

Final Draft

Write the final draft.

Title

Memo

Memo

Essential Guide to Writing

Writing Avenue

Paragraph Writing